*Bryce Canyon National Park is a place long noted for color and shapes. But much more awaits here. In this place one can stand on top of the world and look to the edge of time. Here "as-far-as-the-eye-can-see" still exists. The view is yet unsullied and the sounds of silence prevail.*
*Rest a while and refresh yourself.*

*T*his canyon that is not a canyon, but the intricately
carved edge of the Paursaugunt Plateau,
is best known for its hoodoos. These water-carved walls,
fins and spires reflect the moving sun with
ever-changing colors.

*National park areas
are special landscapes set aside
by acts of Congress to protect
and preserve features of national
significance that are generally
categorized as scenic, scientific,
historical and recreational.*

*As Americans, we are joint
caretakers of these unique places,
and we gladly share them with
visitors from around the world.*

Bryce Canyon was set aside for its
scenery, panoramic views, and
scientific interest and to protect
the area in its natural state.
Wildlife abounds in the park.
Changes in elevation are revealed
in the plants of meadows and
forests. Views as far as 200 miles,
night skies sprinkled with stars
dimmed only when the moon is
full, quiet broken by the song of a
bird or the chatter of a squirrel—
all of these are here for the taking.
Beyond all this, other public lands
form an unparalleled backdrop
and increased opportunities for
enjoying the richness
of southern Utah.

JEFF GNASS

*Bryce Canyon National Park, located in southern Utah, was first set aside in 1923 to preserve an amphitheater of colorful pinnacles, spires, and walls, all carved by erosive weathering.*

*Front cover: Queen's Garden from Sunrise Point, photo by Jeff Gnass. Inside front cover: A winter sunrise, photo by Kaz Hagiwara. Page 1: The Sinking Ship from Bryce Point, photo by Fred Hirschmann. Pages 2/3: Bryce Ampitheater, photo by Larry Ulrich. Pages 4/5: Rainbow Point, photo by Jeff Gnass. Pages 6/7: Silent City at sunset, photo by Larry Burton.*

Edited by Cheri C. Madison.
Book design by K. C. DenDooven.

Fourth Printing, 1994.
in pictures BRYCE CANYON The Continuing Story
© 1989, KC PUBLICATIONS, INC.

LC 89-045016. ISBN 0-88714-032-7.

# in pictures

# Bryce Canyon

## The Continuing Story®

by Susan Colclazer

Susan Colclazer, a native Virginian, has worked her way westward with the National Park Service. Starting in Virginia, she worked in Washington, D.C., Missouri, Colorado, and Arizona (where she met and married her husband) before moving to Bryce Canyon National Park in 1986. English courses at the University of Richmond and natural science studies at Virginia Polytechnic Institute and the University of Virginia supplement her degree in psychology from Westhampton College in Virginia.

# Bryce—A "Canyon" is Carved

The Silent City does speak—of its past. Each carved form shows layers of sediments representing changes in fluctuating lakes of 60 million years ago. Mud, silt, and sand settled to the bottom and in time were cemented by carbonates. The exact composition of each layer depended on the level of the lake, the materials washing in from shore and the life of the lake itself. These sediments covered layers already formed and were in turn covered by younger layers. Some 15 million years ago, earth forces began to lift large blocks to form the plateaus that today are the Grand Staircase. Erosion of the Paunsaugunt Plateau's edge formed Bryce Canyon, revealing those ancient lake deposits and the layers which preceded them.

JOE ARNOLD JR.

▲ **Water seeped into the debris lying along the** slopes. By night it froze, pushing the debris; by day the mass thawed, loosened and was pulled downward by its weight. Freezing and thawing, debris moved downhill, scouring the bases of the vertical faces on the way. Strengths and weaknesses of those ancient deposits give shape to today's hoodoos.

◁ **Here, water attacked the higher block first, eroding** it to become the adjacent valley. Then it started sculpting the exposed edges of the block which we see as today's Paunsaugunt Plateau. Gullies began washing out at weaker spots along the rim of the plateau. Less vulnerable rocks were left as the large vertical walls and formations we call hoodoos.

◁ **E**rosion occurs from within as well as outside the rock. When surface erosion meets a place where materials have been dissolved and removed from inside the rock, "windows" result.

◁ **W**ater running over the harder caprock slides down the cliff face. Sometimes hanging on the underside, sometimes falling to the sill, water gently dissolves the rock surface to expand windows into arches. Natural Bridge, which is really an arch, now spans a drainage which deepens each year with spring runoff and summer rains. Horizontal and vertical cracks, softer and harder rock, chemical and mechanical weathering—all give clues to the future just as the arch tells us of the past.

△ **W**hen the caprock yields before the sides, only two columns remain of an arch. When harder layers are reached, the process starts anew. Broken rock rests on the slopes until water carries it further down the hill.

**B**enches in the Queen's ▷ Garden slow debris in its downhill journey. As the rock breaks down into smaller material and slopes become more gradual, plants are able to take root and grow, further slowing erosion due to runoff. These forces work to both stabilize and change the shape of the land.

△ **From Inspiration Point you can see many phases of erosion. The Table Cliffs in the right** background are the same formation as the Bryce Amphitheater. To the left, the Black Mountains are lava covered portions of the Paunsaugunt. The foreground from left to right shows the phases of erosion that give Bryce Canyon its fame. From the steep slopes of the rim, fins are carved then recarved into numerous closely spaced spires. Older forms lose their height and become rounded. Only mounds of brightly colored dirt remain close to the original edge of the plateau by the Paria River.

***S**lowly, inch by inch, the rim recedes—about a foot* ◁
*in 50 years, studies show. Faster in some places, much
slower in others; faster in wet years, slower in dry ones—
always retreating from the water. Trees and other plants
slow the eroding flow and protect the earth. Then their roots
push against the rock and the rock is broken until it can no
longer support the plants. Downhill, smaller rocks rest on
ever gentler slopes until once again a plant can grow.*

**A gentle** ▷ slope along the Fairyland Trail has been stable enough for this pine to grow. The remains of another remind us that this will not last. Nor will the neighboring rock as its softer pedestal shrinks.

◁ **A** *hike into the canyons will help in understanding what is seen from the rim. As you cross the benches, stop to feel the rock, examine the textures, compare the slopes where different sizes of rock have come to rest. Watch your footing—the pebbles on the trail roll.*

PETER KRESAN

△ **F**rost wedging can enlarge vertical cracks until the weakened rock flakes *off, leaving new surfaces exposed to erosion. Although water usually runs off the sheer faces and drains from the cracks before this can happen, occasionally water is trapped long enough to freeze and refreeze. Once isolated from the main wall, hoodoo shapes are refined by this seasonal sculpting, the mechanical washing away of softer parts and some chemical erosion.*

△ **M**inerals color the white limy formation. Iron oxides from ancient surfaces settled into the forming rock like coloring into a cake to leave the shades of red, pink and orange. Rocks break into smaller and smaller pieces, blending the colors, until small enough to wash away to another place and start the cycle anew.

◁ **P**lants survive a while in this changing environment, then like the rocks, succumb to leave behind a record of the past. Gnarled limbs and exposed roots tell of years combating sliding rock until nourishment is no longer available to sustain life.

**E**rosion takes its toll on man's ▷ works too. In Wall Street, the great flakes fall on the trail. Each spring the winter's rubble is removed by the park's trail crews. Sometimes trails must be closed or even moved.

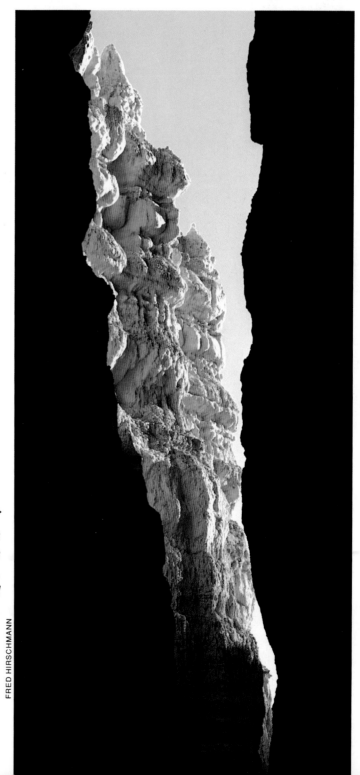

△ **When surrounded by strange shapes and** forms, it seems to be the nature of man to name them—like this formation of "Alley Oop and Dinny." Perhaps it lends familiarity to take away some fear. The Peekaboo Trail is lined with hiding places for the unknown.

**Looking like so many flowers in spring,** ▷ hoodoos seem to have sprouted from slopes of matching colors in the Queen's Garden. In truth, fragments which have fallen and washed down the slopes chisel out the bottoms of the hoodoos.

*Softer layer, harder layer, softer layer—*  *the Queen herself. Named for a statue of Queen Victoria in England, this hoodoo oversees the "garden" in a vigil which will gradually end. Will the queen be gone before a pedestal forms? In our lifetime will we look down on just another capstone covered mound? Will the monarch survive her garden?*

MARK E. GIBSON

FRED HIRSCHMANN

**W**hat part of the hoodoo was the last to fall? *Check the debris at its base and match it to the colors on the spire.*

FRED HIRSCHMANN

*Like an endless game of "Paper, scissors and rock," the snow gently blankets the earth, the sun melts the snow...*

CARLOS ELMER

FRED HIRSCHMANN

◁ **Fins, windows, and columns silhouetted** against a pure sky. Sand, silt and mud dressed in colors of iron. Simple materials made elegant by constant rearrangement. These particles, washed from an ancient landscape to settle in an ancient lake, are removed to settle elsewhere once more.

MARGARET LITTLEJOHN

△ **Shade-tolerant Douglas firs can grow in the** depths of Wall Street. And grow these did to rival the shapes of the rocks as objects of wonder.

◁ **Their covering of rocky soils worn away,** tree roots on tiptoe can be used to measure the rates of erosion.

△ **The Paria River has eroded the plateau in the direction of the stream's head, working** from south to north. Here at Agua Canyon, the land below has already settled and been forested. Even further south in the park, the pink cliffs drop quickly down to the forests, any evidence of past hoodoos washed away by the waters of time.

◁ **Like poorly** laid cement, the "alligator" caps these hoodoos. What event occurred to cause this obviously different layer? Perhaps the lake "turned," leaving a mantle of dolomite-rich deposits, or did the shore recede in some primeval drought?

# Flowers and Animals in Bryce Canyon

The steep slopes are not favorable for life. But, where the slopes settle and above the rim, there is a great variety of plant and animal life. Elevations ranging from 6,000 feet in canyon bottoms to over 9,000 feet at the south end of the park, soils varying with their source rock, moisture retained or drained, sunlight and shadow—all combine to provide a wide range of habitats.

To each habitat some form of life is adapted. Bryce Canyon supports pinyon-juniper, ponderosa, and spruce-fir forests and high meadows. These are home to bear, mountain lion, deer, elk and antelope. With few exceptions none of these larger animals lives entirely within the park. They move freely about the plateau, restricted only by man's continuing developments and conflicting uses of the land.

Coyotes, foxes, and badgers prey on smaller residents including Utah prairie dogs, chipmunks, and ground squirrels. These in turn feed on the grasses, nuts, and berries of the plant communities. Also present are birds, some year-round and some seasonal residents, and insects whose numbers are unknown.

▽ **The hairy stems and yellow flowers of the rabbitbrush spread to meet the sun in open areas** here along the rim and at the forest edges. Small rodents which feed on these plants live in the rocky soils, in crevasses in the rocks and among the tree roots. As you bask in the sun and admire the views, be careful not to disrupt life by trampling plants or feeding the animals.

◁ **Seeking refuge in the rocks, the yellow-**bellied marmot lives on nearby grasses. A true hibernator, the marmot is most active from April until June. After a summer of naps and eating, this rodent begins its long underground stay in August.

MARGARET LITTLEJOHN

GALEN ROWELL—MOUNTAIN LIGHT

**The mule deer is most often** △ seen mornings, evenings and moonlit nights when it browses in the meadows eating grass, leaves and stems of forbs.

MARGARET LITTLEJOHN

◁ **Yuccas grow in the rocky soils** of the meadows and woodlands. Large, globe-shaped, creamy white flowers grace the stalks from April to July and leave grayish, seed-bearing husks in late summer.

**Overleaf:** From dawn to dusk, ▷ throughout the seasons, hoodoos reflect the sun in seemingly endless colors. Photo by Kaz Hagiwara.

23

TOM BEAN

IRENE HINKE-SACILOTTO

▲ *Bluish above, with reddish* bars below, the Coopers hawk makes short flights low over the trees searching for its prey of small birds and mammals.

*The Utah prairie* ▲ dog fared well enough when its predators were hawks and badgers. But, when southern Utah was settled by farmers and ranchers, the rodent's affinity for farm crops almost caused its extinction.

LYNN CHAMBERLAIN

▲ *The badger's long, sharp claws and short, stout body enable it to* dig swiftly and capture small mammals even in their dens. Birds, eggs and reptiles add to its diet.

GLENN VAN NIMWEGEN

**Y**ellow summer flowers yield to the delicate feathery fruits of the salsify. This sunflower grows along the roadside and at meadow edges.

GLENN VAN NIMWEGEN

**B**lue on yellow; damsel fly on cinquefoil. Not all of the colors are in the canyon walls. Here too, among the living things, are cycles as constant as those forming the hoodoos.

MARGARET LITTLEJOHN

**L**ook under ponderosa pines for clusters of the hairy stemmed, leafless pinedrops.

LARRY BURTON

**M**anzanita covers the forest floor. The bell shaped flower turns to a greenish berry or "little apple," providing food for small rodents and other animals.

◁ **T**he white-breasted nuthatch goes down the tree as easily as up. He cocks his head as if looking curiously about. A winter resident, the nuthatch searches for food in cracks in the trees.

MARGARET LITTLEJOHN

◁ **I**n late spring or early summer, wild iris blooms in wet meadows like the one near the visitor center.

LARRY BURTON

GLENN VAN NIMWEGEN

**L**ook closely ▷ for the flowers of the paintbrush. Both leaves and bracts are brightly colored.

MARGARET LITTLEJOHN

◁ **A** lone aspen leaf in the grass tells of a niche high on the plateau or on the north slope of a canyon where both sunlight and water are abundant.

**T**he omnivorous gray fox is seldom
seen. It usually seeks its food of fruits, berries,
rodents and reptiles at night.

**T**rips in the winter sun, searches for food,
dramas of life and death—we can read of them all
in the tracks on the snow.

**T**he mountain lion
ranges far and wide so
none live entirely within the
park. Deer are its primary
food although it will eat
smaller animals or birds.
This elusive cat does well
in southern Utah where
ample public lands provide
adequate range and there
is minimal contact
with man.

▲ **Ebenezer Bryce emigrated from**
Scotland and met and married Mary Ann
Parks in Salt Lake City. They made a
series of moves southward, establishing
sawmills in Utah communities. In the mid-
1870s they moved with their ten children to
homestead near the Paria River.

## Early History of Bryce Canyon

Only isolated artifacts and remnants of hunting camps tell us of earliest man's use of the park area. The Indians of southern Utah lived in the warmer valleys, using the plateaus for hunting and fishing. To the southwest, Paiute farmers used irrigation to supplement the sparse rainfall.

The Spanish Trail came south along the route of today's Highway 89 almost to Panguitch, then turned across Bear Valley and continued south and westward across Nevada in the early 19th century. Later Europeans used this route, bringing their domestic herds. The impacts of both man and beast forever changed the Indian way of life.

Although government surveyors and explorers came close, and some wrote of seeing the "pink cliffs," no records tell of their seeing into the canyons of Bryce.

**Jane Mattice (left) was a daughter** ▽
of Ebenezer Bryce—Sara Bryce
(right) his daughter-in-law.

▲ **Bryce built a road up the canyon to haul timber**
from the plateau. The Bryces farmed and raised cattle
here. In 1880, they sold out and moved to Arizona
leaving the farmstead, one married daughter, and their
name. Today the park and one of the overlooks share
the name of "Bryce's canyon."

△ **Rueben and Minnie Syrett moved from Panguitch to homestead near the canyon's rim in 1916.**
They were enthralled with the canyon. In 1919, Salt Lake City friends talked Ruby into bringing up gear so they could camp in the pines by the rim. Soon "Tourists' Rest" was developed on a school section in the Powell National Forest. Food and supplies were brought up from the homestead four miles south.
In 1923, the Union Pacific Railroad bought Ruby's development in the newly proclaimed national monument, and the Syretts built Ruby's Inn on their own land.

**Railroad** ▷
management realized the importance of good roads for local transportation. They worked with the state and federal governments to get roads built connecting their facilities in Zion, Cedar Breaks, Bryce Canyon, and the North Rim of the Grand Canyon.

NPS PHOTO

*Early road* building required considerable ingenuity and hard work. By 1934, the Civilian Conservation Corps (CCC) was at work in the park further developing the road system, grading and seeding slopes, doing erosion control in meadows, and building trails, campgrounds and fencing.

*Both commercial and private parties visited the canyons along the new roads. Caravans* were a common sight in the early days of the park. Utah Parks Company cars brought visitors from the railroad in Cedar City, part of a trip which included the other park areas.

△ **Legislation to establish the monument as Utah National Park was passed in 1924.** Additional lands were acquired in 1928, and the name was changed to Bryce Canyon National Park. Meanwhile, Union Pacific hired Gilbert Stanley Underwood to plan the lodge, built between 1924 and 1927, and the cabins which were completed by 1929. The Utah Parks Company operated these facilities until they were donated to the park in 1972. TW Recreational Services, Inc. now operates the Bryce Canyon Lodge, a National Historic Landmark.

▽ **CCC crews built the campground roads, established the sites and built the walkway to** the "lecture circle." Logs were hewn for seats. Naturalist talks were given in front of the lodge for years. Today's campground amphitheaters are the site of naturalist programs on summer evenings.

# Winter at Bryce Canyon

Ah, winter. Snow drifts gently through the air, gathering ever gathering, until the land lies white and clear. Little puffs on pine trees wait for a breeze to fling them to the ground. Deer tracks lead to the valley below. Far out on Rainbow Point, a mountain lion leaves four-toed traces of its passing to quicken the heart of a lone skier. The fiery hoodoos are cooled by caps of white snow, while inside fires warm visitors in this special season.

Today you don't have to be a hearty pioneer braving hardships to stay on the plateau. The roads are plowed and the overlooks are open shortly after each snow. Food and lodging are available near the park. Some campsites and backpacking are available in the park all year. Cross-country skiing and snowshoeing are added to hiking as ways to see the park. Follow marked trails, or be the first to make tracks on new-fallen snow.

WILLARD CLAY

△ **The Silent City absorbs**
the quietness of the season
and glows in the low-angled
rays of the winter sun.

GARY LADD

**Visibility is best in winter** ▷
when winds come from less
polluted places. From Yovimpa
Point, the plateau edges step down
the Grand Staircase with views of
up to 200 miles. Here, no higher
forms impede the view into
Arizona and sometimes
even New Mexico.

◁ **Inspiration Point takes on mystical**
qualities and becomes a visual parfait,
layers of snow outlining layers of
the hoodoos.

△ **The name "Fairyland Canyon"** seems especially appropriate and the ways of erosion are clearer when snow outlines the hoodoos. Vertical faces shed snow as the slopes below accumulate it. North slopes hold the snow even as sun melts snow on south slopes.

**Both Inspiration and** ▷ the distant Bryce Point are accessible by car. Compare shaded north faces, little touched by the low rays of the sun, with south slopes which undergo almost daily freeze-thaw cycles.

△ **Massive vertical walls are carved out of the plateau by water running down gullies. When** conditions are right, crevasses that do hold water also succumb to freezing and thawing so that large slabs are pushed off to add to the debris below. The sheer walls hold little water or snow, so erosion is mostly at the bases of the hoodoos. Slope debris is lifted by nightly freezes and loosened to scour the large blocks as it moves downhill. Loose debris is washed out by snow melt and summer rains.

# People Today at Bryce Canyon

Bryce Canyon is a year-round park with most visitors coming in the summer months. Sightseeing by car is easy. Just stop at one of the 13 overlooks, stretch your legs and take in the scenery. A concessioner leads horseback rides along the Peekaboo Loop, and rangers conduct walks, talks and campfires throughout the summer. Some 50 miles of trail invite you to take a longer hike or even an overnight backpack on your own. It is cool in the higher elevations, but a trip into the canyons requires water and long sleeves are recommended to avoid sunburn.

The Bryce Canyon Lodge and park campgrounds are available for overnight stays from late spring through early fall. One loop of the campground is open all year. There's plenty of private camping and lodging just outside the park and in the local communities all year. Plan to spend at least one half day for a quick trip. Plan several days to really see the park.

DICK DIETRICH

◁ *The Bryce Amphitheater trails—Queen's Garden, Navajo Loop and Peekaboo Loop— are the most used. For a less strenuous walk, try the Rim Trail anywhere between Fairyland and Bryce Points or the Bristlecone Trail at Rainbow Point. Under-the-Rim, Riggs Spring and Fairyland trails are longer.*

NPS PHOTO BY R. RAVEN

## Bryce Canyon Natural History Association

The Bryce Canyon Natural History Association, a private, non-profit organization, was founded to assist the interpretive and research programs of the park. Proceeds from the sales of publications and interpretive items have been returned to develop new publications, sponsor special programs, and fund research. Association personnel also help staff the visitor center and provide information and other services to visitors.

Since 1986, the Association has funded remodeling of the visitor center lobby and part of the new wayside and museum exhibits in addition to their own publishing program.

▲ **You don't have to be a Junior** Ranger to join in children's workshops, but you can be one if you do. Younger visitors can also attend the conducted activities and do special projects to help the park. Every summer, rangers explain cultural and natural history in walks, talks, and evening campfire programs available to all. Check at the visitor center for activity times.

RUSS FINLEY

◁ **Staff, a** slide show and exhibits at the visitor center can answer most questions and help you plan your stay. Required backcountry camping permits are available at no cost.

AUDREY GIBSON

FRED HIRSCHMANN

△ **Photography is a favorite activity at any time of year,** and Sunrise Point is a favorite place for photographers. The park is impressive in both color and black and white.

◁ **Fairyland and Paria roads are left** unplowed for cross-country skiing. The Rim Trail offers ample opportunity for going on your own during winter months. Dress in layers. Let someone know when you expect to return, and ski with a partner if you're going far.

**Bryce-Zion Trail** ▷
Rides offers half-and all-day rides from spring through fall. Check at the lodge for times and reservations, then join the wranglers for a ride into the canyon along the Peekaboo Loop. Both new and experienced riders are welcome.

DICK DIETRICH

## The Forest and the Meadows

Plants have only a tenuous hold on the steeper slopes, but forests and meadows grow well both on and below the plateau. Forests grow best where drainage is good, and meadows thrive where water collects. Changes in elevation, precipitation, and sunlight help determine what grows in the forests and meadows.

The drier sagebrush flats covering the lower slopes on the way to Bryce yield to pinyons and junipers where there is adequate water. At 8,000 feet near the entrance to the park, ponderosa forests predominate, then intermingle with shade-tolerant spruce-fir forests at the south end of the park where elevations reach over 9,000 feet. Bristlecone pines cling to the rocky exposures near Rainbow Point where little else can survive.

*GLENN VAN NIMWEGEN*

**G**rasses, flowers and forbs are most common in the wetter meadows. Shrubs and small pines ring the meadow edges seeking sun, while large trees grow on better-drained slopes along the Under-the-Rim Trail. Backpackers have time and solitude to enjoy this other side of Bryce Canyon. Free permits are required for overnight stays along the trails.

*MARGARET LITTLEJOHN*

**A**spens usually grow in clones or clumps with younger trees sprouting from extended root systems. Seeds sprout only in open soil, so fire or some other disturbance is needed to establish new clones. Trees in one clone all leaf out at the same time and share a common color in the fall. Red big-tooth maples provide a colorful contrast to yellow aspen.

JEFF GNASS

**O**lder ponderosa forests
*may bear fire scars from
centuries past. Frequent small
fires can keep the ground below
clear of litter, burning the
needles and other fuel without
damaging the healthy trees.*

GLENN VAN NIMWEGEN

◁ **M**eadows, too, depend
*on natural processes to
maintain a diversity of plants.
Many of the park's meadows
have grown back thanks to
check dams built in the 30s and
50s to stop erosion that began
with overgrazing and
road building.*

43

FRED HIRSCHMANN

▲ **Bristlecone pines, some several thousand** years old, live where other trees cannot. Their twisted forms testify to their basic hardiness. Sometimes harsh conditions—wind, cold, snow, drought—kill parts of the tree leaving only a single branch alive, fed by the remaining roots. Here erosion may be their greatest enemy, exposing roots and depriving the tree of nourishment.

## SUGGESTED READING

BEZY, JOHN. *Bryce Canyon: The Story Behind the Scenery.* Las Vegas, Nevada: KC Publications, Inc., 1980.

BUCHANAN, HAYLE. *Wildflowers of Southwestern Utah.* Bryce Canyon, Utah: Bryce Canyon Natural History Association, 1992.

STROUD, TULLY. *The Bryce Canyon Auto and Hiking Guide.* Bryce Canyon, Utah: Bryce Canyon Natural History Association, 1983.

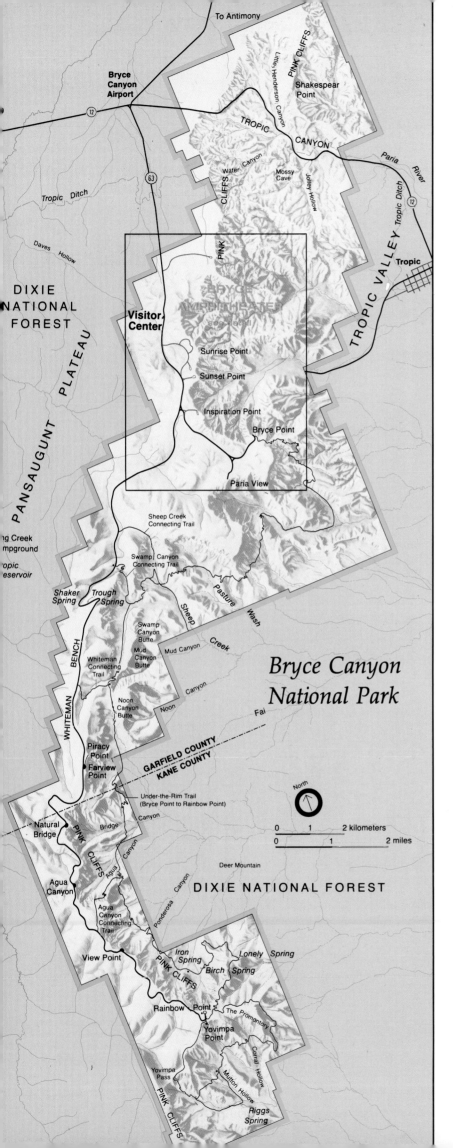

## Bryce Canyon National Park

**Labels on main map (img_1):**

To Antimony

Bryce Canyon Airport

12

63

PINK CLIFFS

Shakespear Point

Little Henderson Canyon

TROPIC

CANYON

Water Canyon

Mossy Cave

Jolley Hollow

Paria River

Tropic Ditch

Tropic Ditch

Tropic Valley

Tropic

Tropic Ditch

Daves Hollow

DIXIE NATIONAL FOREST

PANSAUGUNT PLATEAU

PINK CLIFFS

Visitor Center

BRYCE AMPHITHEATER

Sunrise Point

Sunset Point

Inspiration Point

Bryce Point

Paria View

ng Creek mpground

ropic eservoir

Sheep Creek Connecting Trail

Swamp Canyon Connecting Trail

Shaker Spring

Trough Spring

Swamp Canyon Butte

Mud Canyon Butte

Mud Canyon

Sheep Creek

WHITEMAN BENCH

Whiteman Connecting Trail

Noon Canyon Butte

Noon Canyon

Pasture Wash

Bryce Canyon National Park

Fai

GARFIELD COUNTY
KANE COUNTY

North

Piracy Point

Farview Point

Under-the-Rim Trail (Bryce Point to Rainbow Point)

Natural Bridge

Bridge

Canyon

PINK CLIFFS

Agua Canyon

Agua

Agua Canyon Connecting Trail

View Point

Ponderosa Canyon

PINK CLIFFS

Iron Spring

Birch Spring

Lonely Spring

Rainbow Point

The Promontory

Yovimpa Point

Yovimpa Pass

Mutton Hollow

Corral Hollow

Riggs Spring

PINK CLIFFS

Deer Mountain

DIXIE NATIONAL FOREST

0    1    2 kilometers
0    1    2 miles

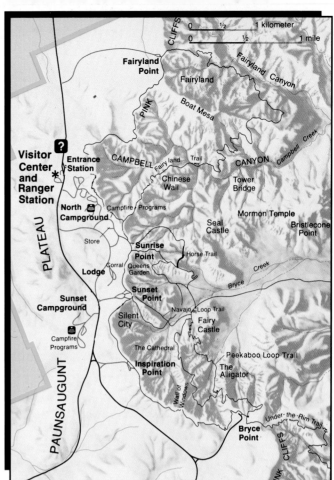

**Labels on amphitheater map (img_2):**

0   ½   1 kilometer
0   ½   1 mile

Fairyland Point

Fairyland

Fairyland Canyon

Campbell Creek

Boat Mesa

PINK CLIFFS

Visitor Center and Ranger Station

Entrance Station

CAMPBELL CANYON

Fairyland Trail

Chinese Wall

Tower Bridge

North Campground

Campfire Programs

Store

Mormon Temple

Bristlecone Point

Seal Castle

Lodge

Corral

Queens Garden

Horse Trail

Bryce Creek

Sunrise Point

Sunset Campground

Sunset Point

Navajo Loop Trail

Fairy Castle

Silent City

Campfire Programs

The Cathedral

Peekaboo Loop Trail

The Alligator

Inspiration Point

Wall of Windows

PLATEAU

PAUNSAUGUNT

Bryce Point

Under-the-Rim Trail

PINK CLIFFS

△ **BRYCE AMPHITHEATER**

◁ **BRYCE CANYON**

▽ **VICINITY MAP**

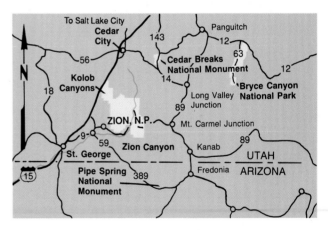

**Labels on vicinity map (img_3):**

To Salt Lake City

Cedar City

Panguitch

143

12

63

56

Cedar Breaks National Monument

12

Kolob Canyons

14

Long Valley Junction

Bryce Canyon National Park

18

89

N

ZION N.P.

Mt. Carmel Junction

9

59

Zion Canyon

Kanab

89

St. George

UTAH
ARIZONA

Pipe Spring National Monument

389

Fredonia

15

***Location:*** *17 miles east of US 89 in southern Utah. Elevations: Visitor Center 8,000 feet. Rainbow Point 9,000 feet. Temperatures: Summer, 40° nights—80° days. Winter, sub freezing to sub zero nights—sub freezing to 50° days.*

FRED HIRSCHMANN

Thor's hammer reflects the first glow of the morning sun. As you add this to your memories, reflect on the ancient times that built the layers of sediments, the earth forces that lifted those sediments to face the sun, the rain and the snow. Reflect on the time that worked with these elements to carve away the weaker layers and the time that it has taken debris moving downhill to scour out these remarkable forms. Consider the land beyond the glow and the people who have passed through here. And in all this, know that Bryce Canyon is not just a place of its past, nor is it a place for only now. Know that Bryce is also a place of the future. Know that we are now a part of its continuing story.

MARK E. GIBSON

▲ **Part of the Sentinel fell in 1987 (compare this picture with the one on page 15).**
*Bryce Canyon is not a static place. Both gullying and exfoliation work to shape this land.*
*Winter and summer, it ever changes. Yet it remains to pleasure our senses.*

**I**nside back cover: *Trees grow* ▷
*tall to reach the sunlight in Wall*
*Street. Photo by Ray Atkeson.*

**B**ack cover: *Boat Mesa is a* ▷
*remnant of younger layers that*
*once covered the area.*
*Photo by Jeff Gnass.*

**Books in this in pictures ... The Continuing Story series are:** Arches & Canyonlands,
Bryce Canyon, Death Valley, Everglades, Glacier, Glen Canyon-Lake Powell, Grand Canyon,
Hawai'i Volcanoes, Mount Rainier, Mount St. Helens, Olympic, Petrified Forest,
Sequoia & Kings Canyon, Yellowstone, Yosemite, Zion.

**Translation Packages are also available.** Each title can be ordered with a booklet
in German, or French, or Japanese bound into the center of the English book.
Selected titles in this series as well as other KC Publications' books are available
in up to five additional languages.

**The original national park series:** The Story Behind the Scenery, covers over 75 parks
and related areas. A series on Indian culture is also available. To receive our catalog
listing over 90 titles:
**Call (800-626-9673), fax (702-433-4320), or write to the address below.**

*Published by KC Publications, 3245 E. Patrick Ln., Suite A, Las Vegas, NV 89120.*

*Created, Designed and Published in the U.S.A.*
Printed by Dong-A Printing and Publishing, Seoul, Korea
Color Separations by Kedia/Kwangyangsa Co., Ltd.